CRAFTY FUN WITH PAPER!

CRAFTY FUN WITH PAPER!

50 fabulous papercraft projects to make yourself

Marion Elliot

ARMADILLO

This edition is published by Armadillo, an imprint of
Anness Publishing Ltd, 108 Great Russell Street,
London WC1B 3NA; info@anness.com

www.annesspublishing.com

If you like the images in this book and would like to investigate using
them for publishing, promotions or advertising, please visit our website
www.practicalpictures.com for more information.

Publisher: Joanna Lorenz
Series Editor: Lindsay Porter
Designers: Peter Laws and Lucy Doncaster
Photographer: James Duncan
Production Controller: Steve Lang

Manufacturer: Anness Publishing Ltd, 108 Great Russell Street, London
WC1B 3NA, England
For Product Tracking go to: www.annesspublishing.com/tracking
Batch: 7083-22894-1127

PUBLISHER'S NOTE
Crafts and hobbies are great fun to learn and can fill hours of rewarding
leisure time, but some points should be remembered for safety and care
of the environment:
• Always choose non-toxic materials wherever possible, for example
paint, glue and varnishes. Where these are not suitable use materials in
a well-ventilated area and always follow manufacturers' instructions.
• Needles, scissors and all sharp tools should be handled with care. Always
use a cutting board or mat to avoid damage to surfaces.
• Protect surfaces from paint and glue splashes with newspapers.
• Although the advice and information in this book are believed to be
accurate and true at the time of going to press, neither the authors nor
the publisher can accept any legal responsibility or liability for any
errors or omissions that may have been made nor for any inaccuracies
nor for any loss, harm or injury that comes about from following
instructions or advice in this book.

CONTENTS

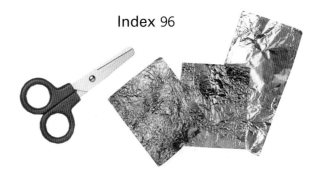

INTRODUCTION

We all use paper every day. Newspapers tell us what is happening in the world; letters bring us news from friends; paper wraps our parcels and fills our books; cardboard protects our food and decorative paper covers our walls. Paper is all around us and life would be very difficult without it!

Paper may be used in other ways too, and this book shows you how to create all kinds of fun objects to use as decoration or to give to your friends. All the projects in this book use paper in its many varieties, and each one shows you what materials to use and how it's done. Some of the projects can be made all by yourself, and others may need an adult's help, but you're sure to want to try them all. Remember, you don't have to copy the projects exactly – you can make up your own items using some of the ideas you've learned. This book is only the beginning, and all you need is paper, a little patience and a big imagination.

Different Types of Paper

Paper in various shades
Lightweight paper is used for projects that involve folding, decoupage and collage among other techniques. Medium-weight and heavy paper are suitable for projects that involve scoring, cutting, printing and folding.

Corrugated cardboard
This is perfect for making armatures for papier-mâché projects. It comes in a variety of thicknesses. Use clean, uncreased cardboard in order to achieve the best results. Good sources of corrugated cardboard are discarded computer and TV boxes or packaging used for posting items bought on the Internet.

Crêpe paper sheets
A very dry-textured, rather stretchy paper, this comes in a wide range of shades and is generally used for wrapping and sculptural effects.

Decorative corrugated card
Corrugated card is less heavy than corrugated cardboard used in the papier-mâché projects. It comes in various shades and its corrugations are used as a decorative feature.

Doll's house paper
Interesting papers are available for decorating doll's houses. They come in a variety of patterns including brick, stone, tile and wood and are very useful for general decorative work. They are available in craft stores.

Graph paper
This is useful for scaling up templates that are given in a reduced size.

Handmade paper
Handmade paper is made in a two-part frame called a deckle and mould. All sorts of things including seeds, plants, hair, glitter, wool, very fine thread and food dye can be added to the pulp to make interesting textures in the paper.

Origami paper
This highly decorated, very vibrant thin paper comes already cut into squares. It is used for making origami projects, but is also good for general decorative work and collage.

Paper ribbon
This comes tightly rolled and is unfurled to give a wide crinkly ribbon that is good for creating stiff bows.

Recycled paper
Now widely available, machine-made recycled paper has a texture rather like blotting paper and is very porous. It generally has an attractive speckled surface owing to the various types of paper in the pulp.

Stencil card
This is usually waxed to prevent it from absorbing water from paint and disintegrating. Transparent plastic stencil film is also available.

Thin card
This comes in a range of shades and is perfect for making items such as hats and masks that will be handled frequently.

Tissue paper
Tissue paper is a very fine, thin paper that appears translucent when held to the light. It can be used in many projects and is especially good for creating stained-glass effects.

Tracing paper
This comes in several thicknesses and can be bought in large single sheets or in pads.

doll's house paper

tracing paper

tissue
paper
sheets

graph paper

stencil card

paper in various shades

thin card

handmade paper

corrugated cardboard

decorative corrugated cardboard

origami paper

crêpe paper sheets

recycled
paper

paper ribbon

Materials and Equipment

Adhesive tape
Clear adhesive tape is good for sticking paper, cord and card.

Cotton string
Cotton string comes in a variety of shades and is useful for binding pages together, stringing beads and making picture hangers.

Eye pins
These are small metal pins with a loop at one end. They are used mostly in jewellery to join items such as earrings together. They can be bought from specialist craft and hobby stores.

Hole punch
Use with adult supervision to make holes in paper for decoration or practical purposes.

Household sponge
This can be cut into small squares and used to apply paint with or without stencils.

Ink pad
Use an ink pad with non-toxic ink to stamp stationery and other paper projects.

Masking tape
Masking tape is paper tape that can be removed once it has been stuck down. It is particularly useful for keeping joints in position while glue dries.

Paintbrushes
Paintbrushes in a variety of thicknesses are used for applying glue and paint.

Paints
These must be non-toxic. Paints are used in several projects, especially for decorating papier-mâché. Cover the work surface with paper when using paint.

Paper clips (fasteners)
Paper clips are very useful for holding small pieces of paper together while you are working on a project.

Paper glue
This must be non-toxic. Paper glue comes in a variety of formats. Perhaps the easiest to use is the solid stick of glue.

Pencils and crayons in various shades
These must be non-toxic. They come in a huge variety of shades and are very useful for decorating all sorts of projects.

Rubber cutting mat
These mats are non-slip and protect work surfaces when cutting paper and card.

Ruler
Use for measuring and drawing straight lines.

Scissors
These should be of the type made specially for children with safe rounded blades.

Sequins
Sequins in various shapes, shades and sizes make very good decorations for paper projects.

Split pins
These are split metal pins that open out to hold pieces of paper together. They should only be used under adult supervision.

Stapler and staples
These should be used under adult supervision. Staples are very useful for holding paper together, especially joints in fairly thick papers and cards.

Strong glue
This must be non-toxic and solvent-free. Strong glue is sometimes used to fix in place heavyweight papers. Adult supervision is required and you should cover the work surface with paper before using.

White glue
This must be non-toxic. Undiluted white glue is very useful for sticking heavy cardboard. Diluted, it can be used for papier-mâché.

household sponge

masking tape

adhesive tape

ink pad

rubber cutting mat

pencils in various shades

cotton string

paper clips (fasteners)

crayons

eye pins

strong glue

darning elastic

ruler

eraser

sequins

scissors

stapler

staples

paper glue

pencil sharpener

sequins

paintbrushes

split pins

hole punch

paints

white glue

TECHNIQUES

Folding

Paper can be folded in a variety of ways to great effect. One of the simplest methods is to fold a sheet of paper into equal sections rather like a concertina. You can hang up the finished design as a decoration.

1 Fold two sheets of paper in contrasting shades into sections about 2.5cm (1in) wide.

2 Fold each piece of paper in the middle to make a semicircle. Under adult supervision, fix the ends of the paper together with a staple.

3 Under adult supervision, join the two semicircles together at the outside edges with staples to form a circle.

Scoring

Scoring is a method of creating fold lines in paper so that it can be creased to appear three-dimensional. Some very elaborate effects can be achieved once the technique has been mastered. Score lines can be made with a pair of scissors, but the blades should always be kept closed, and you should do it under adult supervision.

1 Draw the outline of your shape on heavy paper or lightweight card. Add the fold line.

2 Carefully cut out the shape. Using a pair of closed, round-ended scissors, gently score along the fold line to produce an indentation.

3 Gently fold the shape along the score line. Lightly re-score the line if it doesn't fold easily.

Curling

Thin strips of lightweight paper can be pulled with a pencil to create gentle curls. The curls are especially good for making false beards, moustaches, hair, fur effects and so on.

1 Cut thin strips of paper that are about 1cm (³⁄₈in) wide.

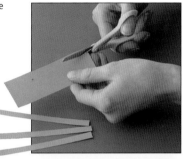

2 Holding a strip of paper in one hand, pull a pencil down its length several times. Don't pull too hard or you'll tear the paper!

3 The paper will form into gentle curls. If you want tighter curling, the strips can be rolled around the pencil rather than just being pulled.

Cutting

Paper may be cut in a variety of ways to make interesting designs. Simple cut-outs are especially good for embellishing greetings cards and decorations.

1 Fold a sheet of paper in half. Make horizontal cuts every 3–4cm (1¼–1½in) down the fold. Open the paper. Push every second fold backwards to make a step effect.

2 Fold a sheet of paper in half. Make slanting cuts every 2–3cm (³⁄₄–1¼in) down the fold. Open the paper. Gently pull down each cut between finger and thumb to make small 'tongues'.

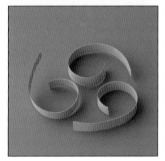

3 Fold a piece of paper in half. Cut half a heart shape at equal intervals down the fold. Open the paper to reveal complete hearts down the length of the paper.

Papier-mâché

Papier-mâché is made by shredding paper, usually old newspapers, and combining it with glue. The paper can be used in a number of ways to make a huge variety of objects both useful and just for decoration.

1 For most projects, paper should be torn into fairly short strips about 2cm (³⁄₄in) wide.

2 Mix non-toxic white glue with water until it is the consistency of pouring cream.

3 Papier-mâché can be pressed into lightly greased forms or wrapped around cardboard armatures, such as this. Leave to dry.

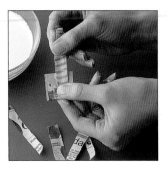

4 To cover smaller shapes, use small, thin pieces of newspaper as you can be more precise with these than you would be with big pieces.

5 Your papier-mâché object may have a slightly rough surface when it has dried out. To make it uniformly smooth, lightly rub the papier-mâché with a piece of fine abrasive paper.

6 Prime your papier-mâché with two coats of non-toxic white paint to conceal the newsprint surface before decorating.

Using Stencils

This is a way of applying decoration to a surface using special card, clear film or metal stencils. A shape is drawn on to the card, cut out, and then paint is applied over the cut-out portion of the stencil with a sponge or brush. It is *possible to buy ready-cut stencils in craft stores or on the Internet, or you can make your own. Ask an adult to cut out your stencil motif for you – craft (utility) knives are very sharp, and are difficult to control.*

1 Cut a piece of stencil card to a suitable size for your stencil and draw your design.

2 Ask an adult to cut out the image from the stencil card using a craft knife and a cutting mat.

3 Mix paint in a palette or on an old saucer. Add a little water to make a slightly sticky consistency.

4 Carefully cut a piece of household sponge into small squares using round-ended scissors.

5 Place the stencil card on a piece of heavy paper or thin card. Dip the sponge in paint and gently dab it over the cut-out motif.

6 Remove the stencil card carefully, one corner at a time, to avoid smudging the paint.

Sponging

This is a way of applying paint to a surface using sponges to give a patchy, holey effect. If you use a variety of sponges with different-sized holes you can make very interesting patterns. Similarly, different shades can be sponged on top of each other if the paint is dry before adding the next shade.

Printing with Foam Rubber Stamps

Simple stamps can be cut from sheets of thin foam rubber and stuck on to cardboard bases. The stamps can be used several times if the excess paint is used up on scrap paper between shades.

1 Cut a piece of household sponge into small squares.

1 To make the stamps, cut several rectangles of heavy cardboard measuring 5 x 3 x 6cm (2 x 3 x 2¼in). Cut an equal number of smaller rectangles from cardboard measuring 1.5 x 3 x 6cm (⅝ x 3 x 2¼in) to form the handles. Stick the handles to the tops of the bases with strong glue.

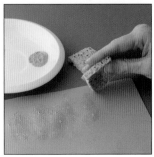

2 Dip a piece of sponge into slightly sticky paint and press it lightly on to a piece of paper of a contrasting shade.

3 When the paint has dried, sponge a second shade on top to make a bright pattern. When dry, the paper may be used to wrap a parcel, as a greetings card or for many other projects in this book.

2 Draw the stamp motif on to foam rubber. Cut it out with scissors and glue it to the cardboard base. Allow to dry thoroughly.

3 Mix a little paint with water to a stiff consistency. Gently dip the stamp in the paint and then press it on to medium-weight paper or thin card.

Tracing

Some of the projects in this book include templates that you can copy when you are creating your paper projects. Tracing is the fastest and simplest way to transfer a template to another sheet of paper.

1 Lay a sheet of tracing paper over the template. Carefully trace over the image with a soft pencil to make a dark line.

2 Turn the tracing over. Scribble over the lines with a soft pencil.

3 Place the tracing the right way up on appropriate paper. Draw over the original lines. When the tracing is removed, the image will have been transferred.

Scaling-up

If you want to make a project larger than the template you can scale it up using graph paper. Use a scale of, say, one square on the template to two squares on the graph paper. You may use a different scale depending on the size you want.

1 If you wish to copy a template that is not printed on a grid, trace it and transfer it to graph paper. If the template you have chosen does appear on a grid, as in this book, proceed directly to step 2.

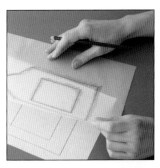

2 Using an appropriate scale, enlarge the template on to a second sheet of graph paper, copying the shape from each smaller square to the larger square.

3 Cut out the new template and transfer it to card or paper.

TEMPLATES

Some of the projects in this book need templates. You can either trace the templates directly from the book, or scale-up to the size required following the instructions given earlier.

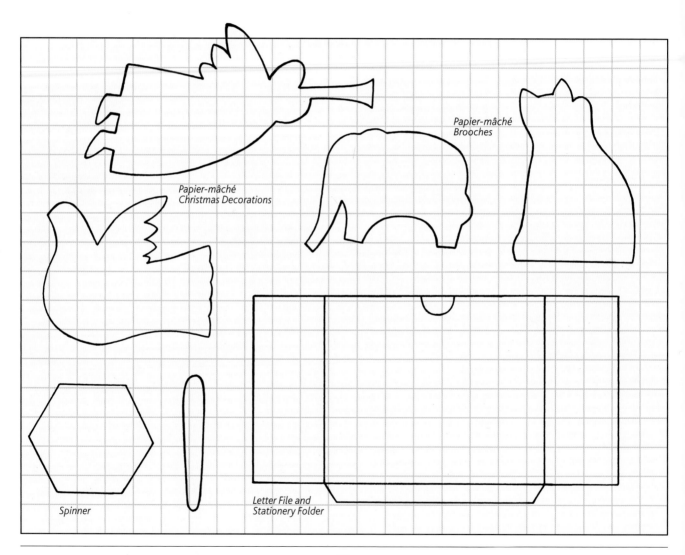

Papier-mâché
Brooches

Papier-mâché
Christmas Decorations

Spinner

Letter File and
Stationery Folder

Christmas Wreath

Dressing-up Doll

Eye Mask

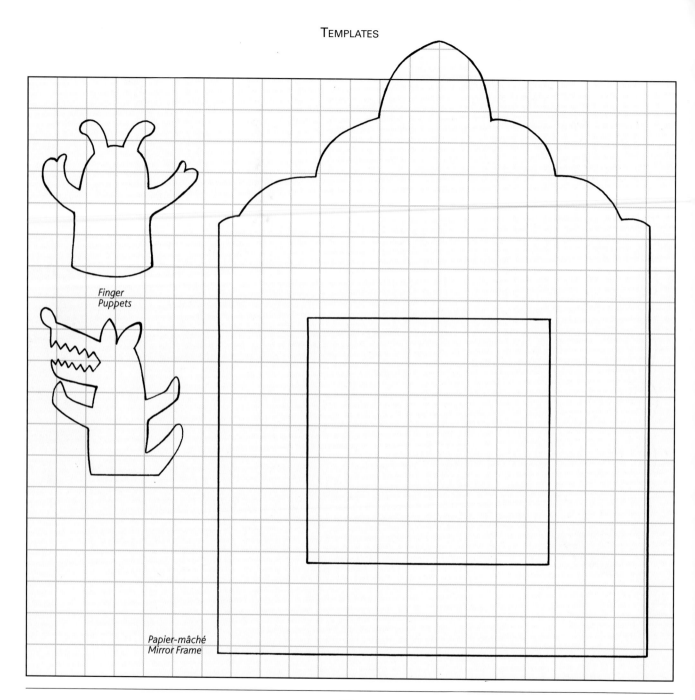

Finger
Puppets

Papier-mâché
Mirror Frame

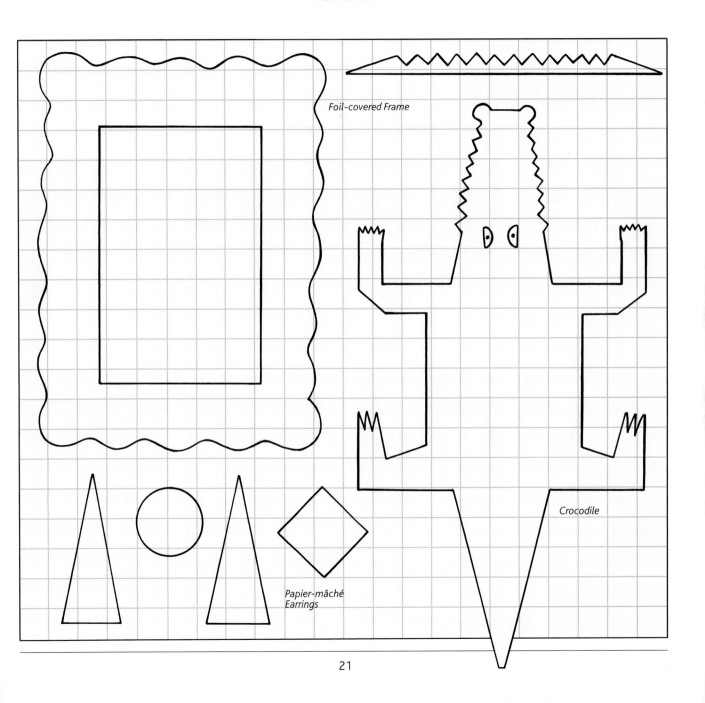

Foil-covered Frame

Crocodile

Papier-mâché
Earrings

Bird Mosaic Tray

This tray will make even the simplest meal look exciting! Mosaic has been used as a decorative device for centuries, and especially fine examples were made by the Romans to decorate the floors of their villas. The look of mosaic has *been imitated here by the use of irregular squares cut from scraps of bright paper. The tray is sealed with several coats of clear varnish so it can be wiped clean with a damp cloth after use to remove any spills.*

YOU WILL NEED
wooden tray
fine abrasive paper
diluted non-toxic white glue
paintbrushes
non-toxic white paint
non-toxic bright paint
scissors
thin paper in a variety of shades
pencil
non-toxic clear gloss
   varnish (optional)

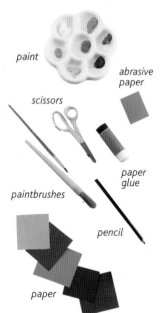

paint

abrasive paper

scissors

paper glue

paintbrushes

pencil

paper

1 Rub down the surface of the wooden tray with fine abrasive paper. Seal the tray with a coat of diluted white glue.

2 Prime the tray by painting it with a coat of white paint and allow to dry completely. This will give a really good finish.

3 Paint the tray with two coats of bright paint, allowing it to dry thoroughly between coats and after you have added the second coat.

4 Cut mosaic squares from sheets of bright thin paper. Dip each in diluted white glue and use a paintbrush to stick in place around the tray.

5 Draw and cut a bird shape from paper and stick it in place in the middle of the tray. Add details cut from contrasting papers and allow the tray to dry overnight.

6 Seal the tray with several coats of diluted white glue or clear gloss varnish, allowing the glue or varnish to dry well between additions.

Painted Postcards

Be original and make your own cards. This ingenious method of applying and scratching off paint gives very professional-looking results, and the cards could be used for place names and invitations to special events as well as for birthday and Christmas cards.

YOU WILL NEED
heavy paper in bright shades
ruler
pencil
scissors
gold paper
paintbrush
non-toxic paint in a variety
  of shades
non-toxic paper glue

paintbrush

gold paper

paint

pencil

ruler

scissors

paper

paper glue

1 Measure and cut out rectangles of bright paper measuring 10 x 3 x 12cm (4 x 3 x 4¾in).

2 Cut slightly smaller rectangles of gold paper.

3 Apply a coat of paint to the gold paper and, while it is still wet, draw a simple design in the paint using a soft pencil. Allow the paint to dry completely.

4 Cut around the scratched images leaving a small border. Stick each of the images on to a rectangle of bright paper with paper glue and allow to dry.

Printed Wrapping Paper

If you don't like the gift wrap you see in stationery stores, print your own using stamps cut from foam rubber. It is very satisfying to be congratulated for both for your choice of wrapping paper and the gift!

YOU WILL NEED
heavy corrugated cardboard
pencil
ruler
scissors
non-toxic strong glue
foam rubber about
  6mm (¼in) thick
non-toxic paint in a variety
  of shades
thin paper in bright shades

paint

strong glue   foam rubber

scissors

corrugated
cardboard

paper

1 To make the stamps, cut several rectangles of heavy cardboard measuring 5 x 3 x 6cm (2 x 3 x 2¼in). Cut an equal number of smaller rectangles measuring 6 x 3 x 1.5cm (2¼ x 3 x ⅝in) to form the handles. Stick the handles to the top of the bases and leave to dry.

2 Draw the image for each stamp on to the piece of foam rubber. Carefully cut around each shape with scissors, ensuring that the edges are smooth.

3 Stick the foam rubber shapes to the base of each stamp and allow to dry thoroughly.

4 Spread a thin layer of paint on to a saucer to act as an ink pad. Press each stamp into the paint, varying the shades as desired, and print the wrapping paper.

Decoupage Frame

Decoupage is a form of decoration using pictures cut from magazines, newspapers, even wallpaper. The pictures are then stuck on to mirror frames, screens and all sorts of objects to make a new and interesting design. Black and white pictures can be hand-tinted with paint that matches or contrasts with the object you are decorating. You can dip the pictures in cold tea to give the paper a pleasing 'aged' effect similar to old photos, or you can shade them with paints.

YOU WILL NEED
painted picture frame
abrasive paper
assorted black and white pictures
scissors
non-toxic paint that matches
   the shade of the frame
undiluted non-toxic white glue
paintbrush
non-toxic clear gloss varnish

frame

abrasive paper

pictures

paint   *paintbrush*

1 Remove the glass and backing from the picture frame. Lightly rub down the paint with abrasive paper to give a patchy, antiqued effect.

2 Trim the pictures, leaving a slight border around the edges.

3 Make a thin solution of paint and dip each cut-out briefly into it until the paper is stained. Leave the cuttings flat to dry.

4 Arrange the dried cut-outs around the frame. When you are pleased with the composition, stick them in place with white glue.

5 Seal the frame with three or four coats of gloss varnish. Leave to dry.

6 Fit your picture inside and replace the glass and backing.

Woven Paper Cards

Paper weaving is a fun way to achieve exciting effects from a very simple process. Pick the papers you use with care so that the shades complement each other, or contrast in interesting ways. You can use the weaving as a design on its own, or mount it behind shaped frames to make unusual greetings cards.

1 Draw a rectangle measuring 16 x 3 x 24cm (6¼ x 3 x 9½in) on medium-weight green card and cut it out. Draw a line down the middle of the rectangle and, with adult help, gently score along it with scissors to form a fold.

YOU WILL NEED
medium-weight card in
  a variety of shades
ruler
pencil
scissors
heavy paper in a variety
  of shades
non-toxic paper glue

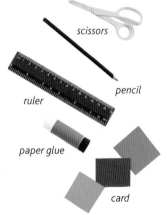

scissors

pencil

ruler

paper glue

card

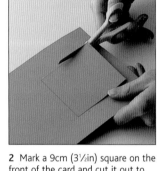

2 Mark a 9cm (3½in) square on the front of the card and cut it out to form a window.

3 Cut a piece of red card measuring 10 x 3 x 10cm (4 x 3 x 4in). Make vertical cuts every 1cm (⅜in) down the card, from just below the top edge almost to the bottom, but do not cut all the way through.

4 Cut several strips of orange paper about 1cm (⅜in) wide.

5 Weave the orange strips through the red to make a checked pattern, as shown. Trim and attach the orange strips at each side of the card with paper glue.

6 Continue in this way until you have a woven square. Stick the woven square to the inside front of the card so that it shows through the window.

Spinner

An alternative to the traditional wooden die is this spinning hexagonal version. You could make it with more sides and higher numbers to make board games more exciting. You will need to use simple geometry if you want to make an eight or ten-sided shape.

YOU WILL NEED
tracing paper
pencil
medium-weight card
scissors
thin red paper
thin blue paper
non-toxic paper glue
scraps of bright paper
thin bright card

scissors

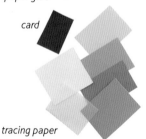
paper glue   pencil

card

tracing paper

paper

1 Carefully trace the spinner from the template in this book and transfer it to the medium-weight card.

2 Cut out the spinner shape and draw around it on red and blue paper. Cut out the shapes you have drawn and stick them to the front and back of the card.

3 Cut thin strips of orange paper and stick them to the red side of the spinner in a star formation to give six sections. Draw the numbers 1 to 6 on scraps of bright paper, cut them out and stick them in sequence around the spinner.

4 Draw and cut a spinning stick from thin bright card. With adult help, make a small slit in the middle of the spinner and insert the stick through the slit.

Calendar

Picture postcards are an ideal source of attractive images that can be used to decorate a calendar. Remember to choose your picture with care and use one that you particularly like – perhaps a holiday destination – because you'll be looking at it for a whole year!

YOU WILL NEED
medium-weight card
ruler
pencil
scissors
green and orange paper
non-toxic paper glue
picture
small calendar
hole punch
thin cord

hole punch
scissors

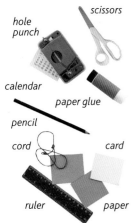
calendar
paper glue
pencil
cord
card
ruler
paper

1 Measure and cut out a rectangle 15 x 3 x 24cm (6 x 3 x 9¼in) from the card.

2 Cut a piece of green paper the same size and stick it on the card.

3 Cut two strips of orange paper 3 x 3 x 15cm (1¼ x 3 x 6in). Cut triangles from one edge of each strip of paper to make a zigzag pattern. Stick these at the top and bottom of the board.

4 Cut your chosen picture to size and stick it in place on the card. Stick the calendar below it. Punch holes in the top of the card and tie cord through the holes to form a hanger.

Paper Chains

One of the quickest and most effective ways to transform a room for Christmas is to make garlands of bright paper chains. Crêpe, shiny or novelty papers all make very fine decorations. As an alternative, why not use different-toned newspapers for unusual recycled paper chains?

YOU WILL NEED
thin paper in a variety of shades
ruler
pencil
scissors
non-toxic paper glue
stapler

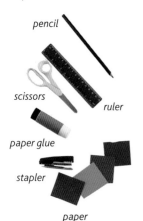

pencil

scissors

ruler

paper glue

stapler

paper

1 Cut paper in a range of shades into strips measuring 2.5 x 3 x 16cm (1 x 3 x 6¼in).

2 Cut narrow strips of contrasting paper 16cm (6¼in) long.

3 Using paper glue, stick the contrasts to the paper strips. Allow them to dry.

4 Bend a decorated strip into a circle and, with adult help, staple the ends together. Interlock a second strip of paper through the first, and again staple the ends. Continue to form a chain.

Christmas Decorations

These decorations, based on snowflake formations, will really brighten your tree with their vivid shades, and they're so much cheaper than glass baubles! Make an especially large and vibrant design for the top of the tree.

YOU WILL NEED
medium-weight paper in a
 variety of shades
ruler
pencil
scissors
paper ribbon
stapler
non-toxic paper glue

pencil

scissors

ruler

stapler

paper glue

paper ribbon

paper

1 Cut four strips of paper each measuring 15cm (6in) long and about 1cm (⅜in) wide. Cut a length of paper ribbon to make a hanger for the decoration.

2 Place the strips of paper in a star formation. Make a loop with the paper ribbon and place it in the middle of the star. With adult help, staple the strips and ribbon together.

3 Carefully snip each strip of paper up the middle to within 1cm (⅜in) of the middle of the decoration. Roll the resulting thin strips of paper around a pencil to curl them.

4 Cut small circles of contrasting paper and stick them at the middle of the decoration to hide the staple.

Christmas Wreath

Celebrate the festive season with this Christmas wreath. The leaves are lightly scored so that they have a three-dimensional effect. Use gold paper to impart an extra sparkle to the musical angel.

YOU WILL NEED
heavy red paper
ruler
pencil
scissors
tracing paper
green, white, gold and pink paper
small stapler
non-toxic paper glue
paper ribbon
thin cord

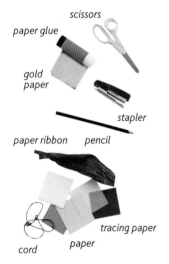

scissors

paper glue

gold paper

stapler

pencil

paper ribbon

tracing paper

cord   paper

1 Draw a circle measuring 24cm (9½in) in diameter on a square of heavy red paper. Cut it out.

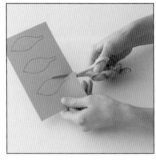

2 Trace the leaf shape from the template and transfer it to the green paper. Cut out about 30 leaves.

3 To make the leaves appear three-dimensional, ask an adult to help you score the middle of each one with a pair of scissors and curve the paper. Score half the leaves on the front and half on the back, so that they curve around the right- and left-hand sides of the wreath.

4 With adult help, staple the leaves around both sides of the wreath, overlapping them slightly.

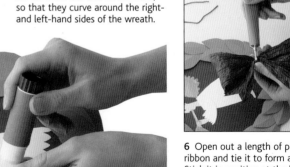

5 Trace the angel pieces from the template and transfer them to white, gold and pink paper. Cut out each of the pieces, and stick them in place on the front of the wreath.

6 Open out a length of paper ribbon and tie it to form a bow. Stick it in position at the bottom of the wreath. Stick a loop of cord to the back to form a hanger.

Papier-mâché Christmas Decorations

These Christmas decorations are fun to make and will look special on your Christmas tree. They make great gifts, too. They could simply be painted as an alternative to sponging if you prefer a smooth finish.

YOU WILL NEED
tracing paper or graph paper
heavy corrugated cardboard
pencil
scissors
newspaper
diluted non-toxic white glue
paintbrushes
non-toxic white paint
non-toxic dark red and
 gold paints
small sponge
darning needle
non-toxic strong glue
eye pins
gold cord

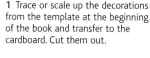

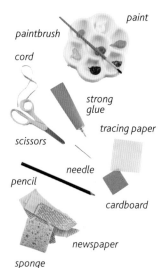

1 Trace or scale up the decorations from the template at the beginning of the book and transfer to the cardboard. Cut them out.

2 Cover each cardboard shape with three layers of papier-mâché. Let them dry overnight.

3 Prime the decorations with two coats of white paint.

4 Paint the decorations dark red. Add a second coat of paint if necessary, so that no white paint shows through.

5 Dab gold paint over each decoration with a sponge to give a mottled pattern.

6 With adult help, make a hole in the top of each decoration with a darning needle. Dab a little strong glue over the hole and push in an eye pin. When the glue has dried, tie a length of gold cord through the eye pin.

Cork Place Mats

Make mealtimes fun with these bright place mats. They are decorated with vibrant turtle motifs cut from paper – but you can make a set with additional animal designs. The mats can't be washed, but they can be wiped clean with a damp cloth after use.

YOU WILL NEED
cork place mats
non-toxic clear gloss varnish
paintbrush
non-toxic bright paint
pencil
thin paper in a variety of shades
scissors
non-toxic white glue

paint

place mat

paintbrush

pencil

scissors

paper

1 Seal the cork mats with a coat of dear gloss varnish and allow them to dry for a couple of hours.

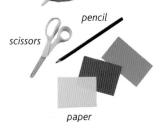

2 Prime the mats with two coats of bright paint and allow them to dry completely overnight.

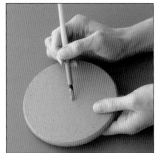

3 Draw each piece of the turtle motif on bright paper and cut out.

4 Apply a coat of white glue to the back of each piece of paper and stick it in position on the mat. Brush over the paper with white glue. When the mat is dry, seal it with several coats of varnish.

Rubber-stamped Stationery

If you're looking for unusual stationery, why not cut stamps from small erasers to decorate writing paper and envelopes? You could press them on to different-toned ink pads or into bright paint to make your own personal stationery. You must ask an adult to cut the eraser for you – craft (utility) knives are very sharp.

YOU WILL NEED
medium-weight paper in
  a variety of shades
ruler
pencil
scissors
paper ribbon
stapler
non-toxic paper glue

ink pad

pencil

erasers

writing paper

1 Draw your design on to the face of the eraser.

2 Ask an adult to trim carefully around the design with a craft knife to leave a raised image.

3 Gently press the eraser on to the ink pad. Test it first on a scrap of paper to make sure that enough ink has been absorbed to make a dark image.

4 Press the eraser firmly on to the writing paper. Remove it carefully to avoid smudging the ink.

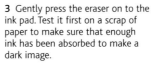

Stencilled Frieze

Print your own frieze using card stencils. Paint is applied through the stencils with small sponges to give a patchy, mottled effect. Re-tell your most-loved tale on a frieze – this one depicts the animals fleeing to Noah's Ark to escape the flood waters. You must ask an adult to cut out the stencils for you – craft (utility) knives are very sharp.

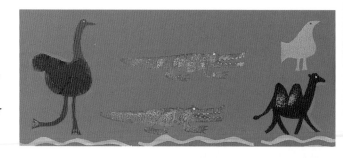

YOU WILL NEED
thin card in a bright shade
ruler
pencil
scissors
stencil card
craft knife
non-toxic paint in a variety
  of shades
palette or old china saucer
squares of household sponge
non-toxic paper glue (optional)

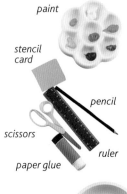

paint

stencil card

pencil

scissors

ruler

paper glue

sponge

card

saucer

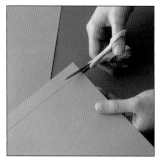

1 Measure and cut out a length of thin card 25 x 3 x 90cm (10 x 3 x 36in) or two pieces 25 x 3 x 46cm (10 x 3 x 18in).

2 Draw various animal shapes, an ark, clouds and water on rectangles of waxed stencil card.

3 Ask an adult to cut out each stencil for you using a craft knife.

4 Place the stencils in position on the thin card. Squeeze a little paint on to your palette or old saucer. Using a square of sponge, dab paint over the area exposed by the first stencil. Lift the stencil from the card.

5 Continue blocking each stencil using appropriately toned paint. Add a row of clouds at the top of the frieze, and water beneath the animals.

6 Allow the frieze to dry completely, and glue it together if more than one sheet of card has been used.

PAPER PROJECTS

Stained-glass Horse

Here's a simple way to imitate beautiful stained-glass windows. These decorations are most effective when hung at a window as the light shines through the tissue paper, bringing it to life. However, they would look great on a Christmas tree as well.

YOU WILL NEED
black cartridge
(construction) paper
white pencil
scissors
tissue paper in a variety
of shades
non-toxic paper glue
thin ribbon or cord

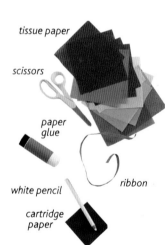

tissue paper

scissors

paper glue

white pencil

ribbon

cartridge paper

1 Draw a horse shape on to black paper with a white pencil. Add star decorations. Cut out the horse shape using scissors.

2 Draw around the shape on a second piece of black paper and cut this out.

3 Using a pair of scissors, carefully cut out the star shapes and features from the first horse. Place this horse on top of the second horse shape and transfer the cut-out motifs with a white pencil. Cut out the decorations from the second horse.

4 Cut small pieces of tissue paper in various shades and stick them to the back of one horse shape over the cut-outs.

5 When all the cut-outs are covered, stick a small loop of ribbon or cord to the top back of the horse.

6 Stick the second horse shape to the back of the first. Using scissors, carefully trim the edges of the horse if necessary.

Monster Feet

Disguise your hands with these wonderful wacky monster feet! They are great fun for parties and, as they cover only the backs of your hands, you will still be able to eat and drink a monstrous amount!

YOU WILL NEED
heavy paper in a bright shade
pencil
scissors
thin paper in contrasting shades
non-toxic paper glue
paper clips (fasteners) (optional)

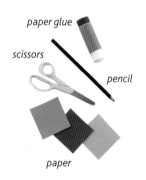

paper glue

scissors

pencil

paper

1 Draw a five-toed monster foot on the heavy paper. Cut it out and use it as a template to make a second foot. Remember to cut an extension of paper from each ankle to form a fastening band.

2 Place the monster feet on thin bright paper. Draw around the tip of each toe and cut out the shapes to make toenails. Stick each toenail to its corresponding toe.

3 Cut out polka dots from a third toned paper. Stick these in position on the fronts of the feet.

4 Wrap the fastening bands around your wrists and ask a friend to mark the point where they overlap. Trim to length if necessary and cut notches to form a fastening, or attach with paper clips.

Crocodile

You can make a whole menagerie of animals by cutting and folding thin card. Split pins are very useful for joining limbs to bodies, since they allow a certain amount of movement in the animals.

YOU WILL NEED
tracing paper or graph paper
pencil
thin blue card
scissors
scraps of white and
   contrasting paper
non-toxic paper glue
black pen
split pins
adhesive tape

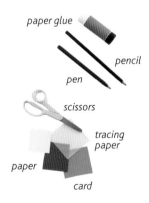

paper glue

pencil

pen

scissors

tracing
paper

paper

card

1 Trace or scale up the crocodile from the template in this book. Transfer the template to the thin blue card. Cut out the body and jaw piece. Cut eye lines.

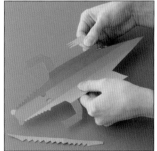

2 With adult help, score the crocodile's body along the dotted lines. Gently bend the crocodile along the scorings to make it three-dimensional.

3 Cut diamonds of contrasting paper and stick them along the crocodile's back. Stick white paper over its eyes, and draw a dot on both using a black pen to represent the pupils.

4 With adult help, make a small slit on either side of the crocodile's head and the jaw piece as indicated. Push a split pin through the slits to fix the jaw to the head. Open the shanks of the pin on the inside of the crocodile and fix in position with tape.

Dressing-up Doll

Shiver me timbers! Here's a brawny brigand for you to dress!
Why not make a parrot to sit on his shoulder and keep him
company on the high seas?

YOU WILL NEED
tracing paper or graph paper
pencil
thin white card
cartridge (construction) paper
scissors
paintbrushes
non-toxic paint in a variety
  of shades

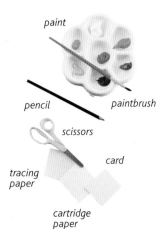

paint

pencil   *paintbrush*

scissors

card

tracing
paper

cartridge
paper

1 Trace or scale up the pirate and his clothes from the template at the beginning of the book.

2 Transfer the pirate to thin card, and the clothes to cartridge paper. Carefully cut them out.

3 Fill in the pirate's features with paint. Paint his underclothes in bright shades and decorate the pirate's clothes.

4 With adult help, lightly score and fold the base of the pirate so that he stands up.

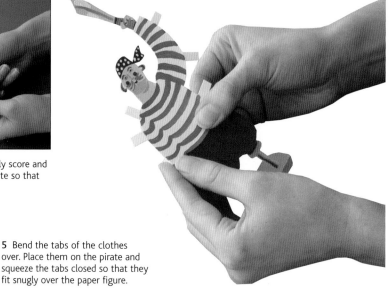

5 Bend the tabs of the clothes over. Place them on the pirate and squeeze the tabs closed so that they fit snugly over the paper figure.

Space Mobile

Join the space race with this lunar mobile! Careful attachment of the suspension threads will ensure that each piece hangs square. You will have to decorate each piece on both sides as the mobile will rotate gently in the breeze.

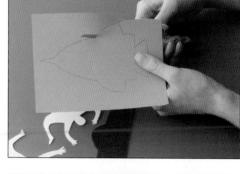

YOU WILL NEED
stiff paper in a variety of shades
pencil
scissors
non-toxic paper glue
darning needle
thin nylon thread

scissors
pencil
paper glue
nylon thread
needle
paper

1 Draw rocket, astronaut and moon shapes on appropriate shades of stiff paper. Cut them out carefully using scissors.

2 Cut decorative additions from scraps of bright paper and stick them on both sides of the shapes.

3 Hold each shape between finger and thumb to test its middle of gravity so that it will hang straight. With adult help, make a hole at this point with a darning needle.

4 Cut lengths of nylon thread and securely tie one end through the hole at the top of each shape.

6 Tie the nylon thread that is attached to the smaller rocket into a loop and use to suspend the mobile. Make sure everything is balanced so that it hangs well.

5 Assemble the mobile. The smaller rocket is the first piece in the structure. With adult help, make a hole in the bottom middle of this piece and hang the larger rocket from it. Make three holes along the bottom of the larger rocket to suspend the astronauts and moon.

Monocle Disguise

Wear this monocle when you want to remain incognito!
It's always good fun to make disguises – let your imagination
run wild and make several for special occasions or festivities.

YOU WILL NEED
medium-weight paper
  in a variety of shades
pencil
scissors
non-toxic paper glue
thin cord
darning needle
thin elastic cord

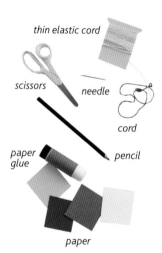

1 Draw nose, moustache, eyebrow and monocle pieces on paper in various shades and cut them out.

2 With adult help, carefully score a central line down the nose to make a fold. Score along the middles of the moustache pieces following the curve and fold them into shape.

3 Assemble the eye and monocle and stick it in place on the nose. Stick the remaining pieces – eyebrows, moustache and monocle cord – in place.

4 With adult help, make two holes in the side of each eyebrow with a darning needle. Push the ends of a length of thin elastic through the holes and knot them, so that the elastic fits your head.

Sun and Moon Masks

Groups of masks on the same theme look very effective when seen together. Make some to illustrate well-known partnerships such as cat and mouse, stars and stripes, or the three wise monkeys.

YOU WILL NEED
heavy blue and yellow paper
pencil
scissors
scraps of thin orange paper
non-toxic paper glue
darning needle
thin elastic cord

scissors

pencil

needle

paper glue

thin elastic cord   paper

1 Draw a moon shape on the piece of blue paper. Remember to make the moon shape large enough to cover half of your face. Cut out the shape with scissors.

2 Cut a star shape from thin orange paper and stick it to the front of the moon shape with paper glue.

3 With adult help, make holes in each side of the mask with a darning needle. Push the ends of a length of thin elastic or ribbon through the holes and knot them so the elastic fits your head.

4 Cut a sun shape from heavy yellow paper. Cut out eye holes and stick small pieces of orange paper to the front of the sun as rays. With adult help, make holes in the sides of the mask and thread through a length of elastic or ribbon. Tie a knot at each end to keep it in place.

Eye Masks

Even if you're not going to a masked ball, you'll have fun making and wearing these disguises! They're especially good if you're in a play or pantomime – you'll be surprised how difficult your friends find it to recognize you!

YOU WILL NEED

tracing paper or graph paper
pencil
thin card in a variety of shades
scissors
paper in a variety of shades
non-toxic paper glue
thin wooden sticks
paintbrush
non-toxic paint
non-toxic strong glue
wax crayons
gold paper

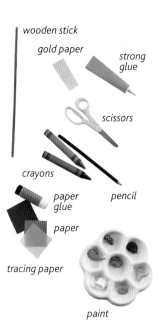

wooden stick
gold paper
strong glue
scissors
crayons
paper glue
pencil
paper
tracing paper
paint

1 Trace or scale up the fiery mask shape from the template at the beginning of the book and transfer it to a piece of orange card. Cut it out with scissors.

2 Place the orange card shape on a piece of purple paper. Extend the sides and top of the eye mask by drawing small spikes, as shown. Cut out this shape.

3 Using paper glue, stick the orange shape in place on top of the purple one. Carefully trim the lower edge of the mask if necessary to give a neat edge.

4 Paint the wooden stick a bright shade. You may have to use two coats of paint.

5 Attach the wooden stick to the side of the mask with strong glue. Stick it the right of the mask if you are right-handed and vice-versa if you are left-handed.

6 To make the leopard mask, use yellow card instead of orange card and apply the spots with wax crayon. The king has a crown made of gold paper, and his eyebrows are applied with wax crayon.

Cowboy Face Mask

Ride the range in this cowboy mask! Wear a bright scarf around your neck for added authenticity and you'll be the envy of every cowpoke in town!

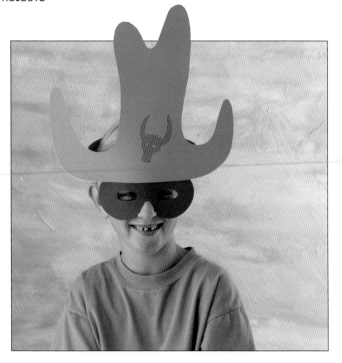

YOU WILL NEED
heavy light blue, dark blue and
   orange paper
pencil
scissors ruler
non-toxic paper glue
adhesive tape
stapler

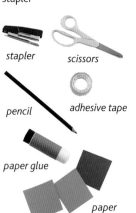

stapler   *scissors*

pencil   *adhesive tape*

paper glue

paper

1 Draw a hat on the light blue paper. Draw a thin band about 5 x 3 x 60cm (2 x 3 x 24in) on the same paper. Cut them out.

2 Draw a steer's head on the piece of orange paper and cut it out Stick the head to the front of the hat with paper glue.

3 Draw and cut out the eye mask from the dark blue paper. Stick it to the back of the hat with some adhesive tape.

4 Stick the hat band to the back of the hat with paper glue. Make sure that it is not visible from the front. To give additional strength, hold the band in place with a strip of tape. Hold the hat band around the head and ask a friend to mark where the two ends overlap. Remove the hat and with adult help, staple or glue the ends neatly together.

Stencilled Snap Cards

A game of snap is always good fun – why not make your own set of cards like this cheerful version? The cards are stencilled with different shades and are bright and simple. Each stencil can be used several times if allowed to dry thoroughly between shades. You must ask an adult to cut out the stencils for you – craft (utility) knives are very sharp.

YOU WILL NEED
stencil card
ruler
pencil
scissors
craft knife
heavy paper in four
    different shades
small squares of
    household sponge
non-toxic paint in four
    different shades
non-toxic paper glue
medium-weight bright card

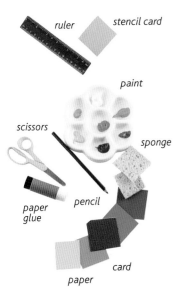

ruler   stencil card

paint

scissors

sponge

paper
glue   pencil

card

paper

1 Cut four pieces of stencil card measuring about 6 x 3 x 9cm (2¼ x 3 x 3½in), using a pair of scissors.

2 Draw four different symbols on the stencil card. Ask an adult to cut out the shapes for you with a craft knife.

3 Cut rectangles of bright paper measuring 6.5 x 3 x 8.5cm (2½ x 3 x 3¼in). Place the first stencil on one of the rectangles. With a sponge square, dab paint over the stencil until the cut-out space is covered. Carefully remove the stencil, taking care not to smudge the paint. Repeat with all the stencils until you have made enough cards.

4 Stick each stencilled rectangle on to a slightly larger piece of medium-weight card. Allow the glue to dry thoroughly before you play snap.

PLAYING SNAP
To play, deal out all the cards to each player. In turn, discard one card on to a central pile. If two cards of the same pair are played in sequence, the first player to notice must shout 'snap' and grab the pair. The player with the most pairs at the end of the game wins. It sounds simple, but try playing very quickly!

Crowns

You'll need a regal bearing to wear these vibrant crowns. Their unusual shape comes from the simple folding and looping of medium-weight paper to very stylish effect.

YOU WILL NEED
medium-weight paper in a
 variety of shades
ruler
pencil
scissors
stapler
adhesive tape
non-toxic paper glue

pencil

ruler

scissors

stapler

paper glue

paper

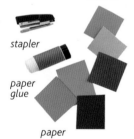

1 Measure and cut out a large rectangle 19 x 3 x 60cm (7½ x 3 x 24in) from medium-weight paper.

2 Mark a point 7cm (2¾in) from the bottom of the rectangle. Draw a central line from side to side. Draw a vertical line from the top of the rectangle to this line every 2cm (¾in).

3 Carefully cut down these lines stopping at the lower horizontal line. Cut off the final strip of paper to make a fastening tab.

4 Carefully bring down each strip of paper to form a loop and with adult help, staple the loops to the remaining strip of paper. Continue all the way around the crown. Bend both ends round to meet and staple and tape the crown at the join.

5 Cut a strip of paper 6 x 3 x 58cm (2¼ x 3 x 23in) from paper of a contrasting shade. Draw a central line dividing the strip in half. Make small notches along one edge of the strip up to the central line. Stick this around the base of the crown, folding the notched edge to the inside of the crown, to form a band.

6 Cut ovals of bright paper to represent jewels and stick them around the crown.

Dotty Notebook

This small notebook is just the right size to carry around in your pocket. You could scale up the dimensions to make a set of notebooks in various sizes, and use them as sketch pads, telephone and address books or diaries.

YOU WILL NEED
medium-weight card
ruler
pencil
scissors
wrapping paper
non-toxic paper glue
thin green paper
non-toxic strong glue
small pad of paper

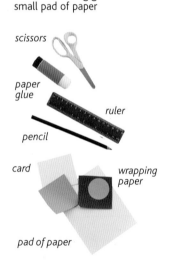

scissors

paper
glue

ruler

pencil

card

wrapping
paper

pad of paper

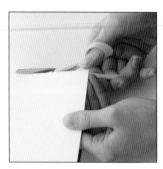

1 Measure a rectangle 12 x 3 x 29cm (4¾ x 3 x 11½in) on the sheet of card and cut it out.

2 Measure two points 14cm (5½in) from the bottom and the top of the card. Draw two lines across the card at these points to leave a central thin space 1cm (⅜in) wide, or slightly wider than the thickness of the pad. With adult help, carefully score along these lines to make two folds.

3 Cut a rectangle measuring 17 x 3 x 32cm (6¾ x 3 x 12½in) from the wrapping paper. Apply paper glue to the back of the paper. Bend the card cover along the fold lines and place the back flap on the paper. Bring the remaining paper over so that it sticks to the board.

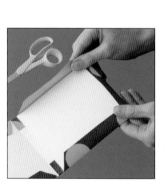

4 Clip the corners of the paper and turn them inside to cover the edges of the notebook cover.

5 Cut a rectangle from the green paper measuring 11.5 x 3 x 28cm (4½ x 3 x 11in). Apply glue. Stick to the inside of the book, covering the edges of the wrapping paper.

6 Apply strong glue to the back of the paper pad and stick it in place inside the notebook cover.

Finger Puppets

Finger puppets are quick and easy to make, and are especially good for entertaining very young children at bed time. If you make familiar characters from books, you can perform short plays to accompany fairy stories and folk tales.

YOU WILL NEED
tracing paper
pencil
medium-weight paper in
  a variety of shades
scissors
non-toxic paper glue

pencil

paper glue

tracing paper   *scissors*

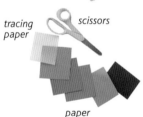

paper

1 Trace the pig and wolf shapes from the templates in this book. Transfer the wolf to orange paper and the pig three times to pink. Cut out each animal.

2 Cut eyes and noses for each animal from small scraps of bright paper and stick them in place with some paper glue.

3 Cut a small strip of paper about 2cm (¾in) wide and long enough to fit around your fingers for each puppet. Stick each animal in the middle of a strip.

4 Securely stick the ends of each finger band together. Allow the puppets to dry thoroughly before playing with them. You can make all sorts of animal puppets in this way.

Magnetic Fish Game

This is a version of an old and much-loved game that has been played by generations of children. To make the game more competitive, you could write a score on the back of each fish. The player with the highest score wins.

YOU WILL NEED
scraps of heavy paper in
    bright shades
pencil
scissors
wax crayons
paper clips (fasteners)
thin wooden sticks
thin, bright cord
small horseshoe magnet

scissors

pencil

magnet   *cord*

              paper clips

*wooden
stick*

        paper

crayons

1 Draw fish shapes on to the scraps of paper and cut them out.

2 Decorate the cut-out fish using wax crayons.

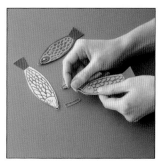

3 Attach a paper clip to the nose of each fish so that it can be picked up by the magnet on the end of the fishing line.

4 To make the fishing rod, tie a length of cord to the wooden dowel and tie a small magnet to the end of the line.

Horse Tableau

This desert scene could be used as a decoration for a party spread. You could make smaller versions for each individual place setting for exciting and unusual table adornments.

YOU WILL NEED
yellow card
pencil
ruler
scissors
heavy paper in a variety
  of shades
adhesive tape
non-toxic paper glue

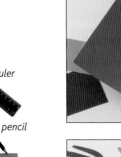

ruler

scissors

pencil

card

paper

1 Draw a rectangle measuring 15 x 3 x 20cm (6 x 3 x 8in) on yellow card. Cut it out.

2 Draw a horse shape on a piece of brown paper. Draw a cactus and a strip of grass on a piece of green paper. Draw another cactus on a piece of red paper. Carefully cut out all of these shapes using scissors. Add the horse's features with scraps of bright paper, as shown in the main image.

3 Cut small circles of bright paper and snip around the edges to make bright 'flowers'.

4 Mark where the horse and cacti will stand on the yellow card. With adult help, make thin slits in the card at these points using a pair of scissors. You may need adult help.

5 The horse, cacti and strip of grass should be scored, with adult help, to make tabs about 1cm (³⁄₈in) wide. Fold over each tab, and insert the horse and cacti in the appropriate slits in the yellow card. Stick them in position.

6 Stick the flowers on the yellow card around the horse and cacti and stick the strip of grass along the front of the card.

Noughts and Crosses

This old classic, also known as Tic-Tac-Toe, has been brought up to date with bright jazzy shades. You could make this a portable game for journeys and holidays – use some scraps of card to form a small carrying case for the board and cards.

YOU WILL NEED
medium-weight card
ruler
pencil
scissors
thick pink, yellow, green
   and blue paper
non-toxic paper glue

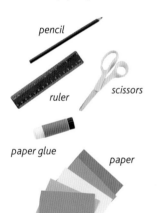

pencil

ruler   scissors

paper glue

paper

card

1 Mark out a square measuring 20 x 3 x 20cm (8 x 3 x 8in) on a piece of medium-weight card. Cut out the square.

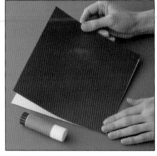

2 Place the cardboard square on the pink paper and draw around it. Cut out the paper square and stick it to the card.

3 Cut a smaller square of card measuring 15 x 3 x 15cm (6 x 3 x 6in). Cut a piece of yellow paper the same size.

4 Stick the yellow paper to the card and cut the card into nine squares each measuring 5 x 3 x 5cm (2 x 3 x 2in).

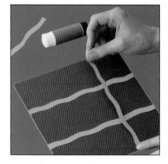

5 Cut four strips of green paper 15 x 3 x 1cm (6 x 3 x ³⁄₈in). Stick them to the pink board to form nine equal squares.

6 Draw noughts and crosses (X's and O's) on the pink and blue paper. Cut them out with scissors and stick them to the yellow squares to complete the cards.

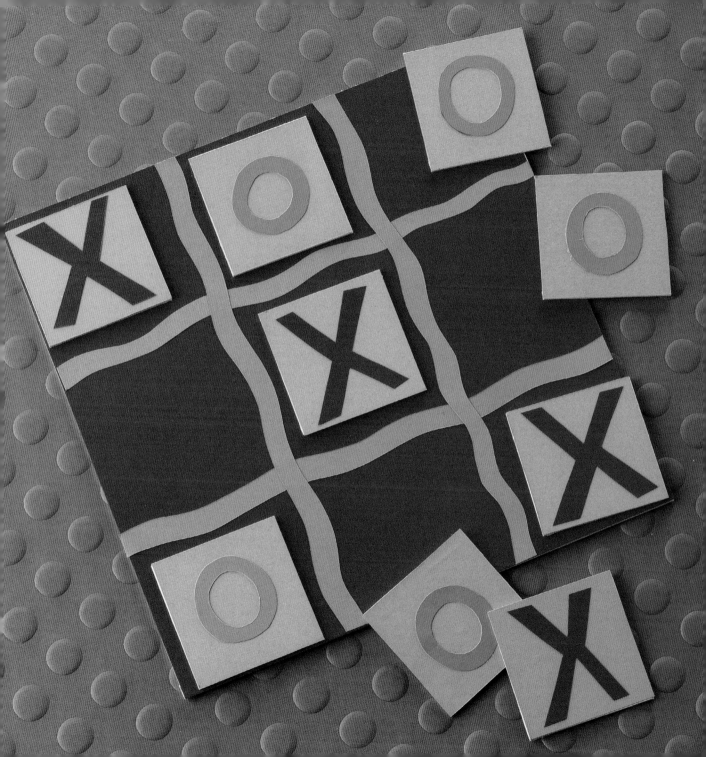

Garden Hat

You'll be the star of the garden party in this lovely, leafy hat.
Add butterflies for extra excitement!

YOU WILL NEED
thin green card
ruler
pencil
scissors
heavy paper in a variety of shades
non-toxic paper glue

1 Draw a rectangle measuring 22 x 3 x 60cm (8¾ x 3 x 24in) on green card. Using the photograph as a guide, mark out the hat on the card. The triangles along the front of should be drawn to varying lengths as they form the stalks of the flowers.

pencil

ruler

scissors

paper glue

card

paper

2 Cut out the hat shape using scissors, remembering to cut the stalks to different lengths. Next, begin to make the flowers. Using scissors, cut circles of heavy paper in various bright shades.

3 Snip small pieces of paper from around the edges of each circle to make petal shapes. Decorate each flower with details cut from contrasting paper, and stick in position using paper glue.

4 Cut butterflies from bright paper and add their markings with scraps of bright paper.

5 Stick the flowers and butterflies around the hat.

6 Hold the hat around your head and ask a friend to mark where the two ends of the hat band meet. Cut a notch in each end of the band to form a fastening.

Jigsaw Puzzle

Puzzles are a great source of enjoyment for many people. This one is cut into simple wavy pieces that slot neatly together. You could make small puzzles and give them as combined greetings cards and presents.

YOU WILL NEED
heavy card
ruler
pencil
scissors
stiff paper in a variety of shades
non-toxic paper glue
hole punch
craft (utility) knife (optional)

hole punch

pencil

ruler

scissors

paper glue

card

paper

1 Measure and cut out a piece of card 20 x 3 x 24cm (8 x 3 x 9½in) using a pair of scissors.

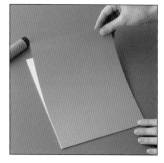

2 Place the card on a sheet of stiff blue paper and draw around it. Cut out the blue paper and stick it to the card.

3 Cut a fish shape from yellow paper and tail pieces from orange. Cut scale shapes from red and orange paper. Cut shells from different shades.

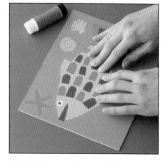

4 Stick the scales and other additions to the fish, then stick the fish to the card. Stick the shells to the background.

5 Cut a strip of purple paper to the same width as the card. Trim the edges into a wavy pattern and make a decorative pattern with the hole punch. Stick the water on the card.

6 Draw nine uneven sections on the back of the board. Carefully cut along the lines with a pair of scissors, or ask an adult to cut using a craft knife.

Cat Papercut Picture

The ancient art of papercutting has been practised in Eastern countries for many years. Make your own decorative cuts and mount them on sheets of contrasting paper. Papercuts make very good gifts, and names and dates of birth can be incorporated into the design. You must ask an adult to cut around the design for you as craft (utility) knives are very sharp.

YOU WILL NEED
heavy paper in various
  contrasting shades
pencil
craft knife
scissors
non-toxic paper glue

pencil

paper
glue

scissors

paper

1 Draw your chosen design on one sheet of bright paper.

2 Ask an adult to carefully cut the excess paper from between the pencil lines to form a framework rather like a stained-glass window.

3 Using scissors, carefully cut a wavy decorative edge around the finished papercut.

4 Cut the second piece of bright paper slightly larger than the picture. Apply glue to the reverse of the papercut and stick it to the contrasting paper.

Rolled Paper Beads

Simple, effective adornments can be made by rolling strips of jazzy paper around a pencil. The resulting beads can be used to make necklaces or bracelets.

YOU WILL NEED
decorative paper
ruler
pencil
scissors
non-toxic paper glue
thin cord

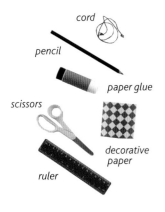

cord

pencil

paper glue

scissors

decorative paper

ruler

1 For each paper bead, cut a strip measuring 4 x 3 x 30cm (1½ x 3 x 12in) from a sheet of decorative paper using scissors.

2 Draw tapering lines along each strip of paper so that it measures 1cm (⅜in) at one end and 4cm (1½in) at the other. Cut away the excess paper.

3 Take a pencil. Wrap the wider end of a paper strip around it. Dab a little glue on the end of the strip and carefully roll the paper around the pencil to make a tubular bead. Glue the narrow end of the strip around the bead, allow to dry, and slip it off the pencil.

4 Repeat the process with the remaining strips to form more beads and when you have enough, string them on to a length of brightly toned cord.

Paper Flowers

These everlasting blooms are made by folding and cutting squares of bright paper into a variety of shapes. Experiment with the technique to make some really fabulous flowers!

YOU WILL NEED
thin paper in bright shades
ruler
pencil
scissors
non-toxic paper glue
non-toxic strong glue
pipe cleaners

pencil
ruler
scissors
paper glue
pipe cleaners
paper

1 Cut squares of bright paper measuring 10 x 3 x 10cm (4 x 3 x 4in). Fold each one into quarters.

2 Cut a curve into each folded square so that it will form a circle when opened.

3 Cut a variety of petal shapes into the curved shape. Open out each flower carefully.

4 Cut circles and other details from contrasting paper and stick them to the middle of each flower.

5 Using strong glue, stick a pipe cleaner to the back of each paper flower to make a stem. You can make stems of different lengths if you prefer.

6 Cut leaf shapes from green paper. Stick these to short lengths of pipe cleaner with strong glue leaving a 3cm (1¼in) 'stem' below each leaf. Wrap this short stem around the main stem of the flower to attach the leaves. Arrange the flowers in a vase or another suitable container.

Recycled Paper Greetings Cards

Recycled paper has an appealing, pitted surface that can be very decorative. These cards are collaged from a mixture of different-toned papers torn from a writing block.

YOU WILL NEED
recycled bright paper
ruler
pencil
scissors
non-toxic paper glue

scissors

ruler

paper glue

pencil

paper

1 Take a sheet of recycled paper and draw a rectangle measuring 13 x 3 x 26cm (5¼ x 3 x 10¼in). Cut out the shape and fold it in half to make a card.

2 Take a sheet of contrasting paper and tear a heart shape out of it.

3 Cut a square of paper in a third shade measuring 12 x 3 x 12cm (4¾ x 3 x 4¾in). Fold it in half. Carefully tear out the middle to leave a ragged border.

4 Using paper glue, stick the square border on the front of the folded card. Stick the heart motif in the middle. You can create additional motifs by tearing designs from bright paper and sticking them on to cards.

Fold-out Greetings Card

Fold-out cards are very versatile – they could simply be decorative like this one, or serve a practical purpose as well. For example, you could cut the words 'Please Come to my Party' from bright paper and stick them to the third panel to make an unusual and exciting invitation.

YOU WILL NEED
blue medium-weight card
pencil
ruler
scissors
thin paper in a variety of shades
non-toxic paper glue

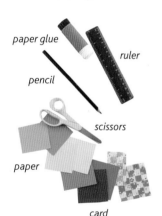

paper glue
ruler
pencil
scissors
paper
card

1 Draw a rectangle measuring 36 x 3 x 20cm (14 x 3 x 8in) on the card. Cut it out.

2 Measure a point every 9cm (3½in) along the top and bottom of the card. Draw three vertical lines and, with adult help, lightly score along them to make three folds. The first and third lines should be scored on the front of the card and the second on the back.

3 Draw and cut out the pieces of each character from papers in various shades.

4 Carefully stick the figures in position on each panel of the card using paper glue.

Photograph Album

Keep your photographs in this album and make more pages as you need them – the cords can be untied to add new leaves. The album could be used to make a commemorative record of a special event such as a wedding or christening, and given as a present.

YOU WILL NEED
medium-weight card
ruler
pencil
scissors
pad of A4 (11¾ x 3 x 8½in)
  recycled paper
hole punch
non-toxic paper glue
thin cord

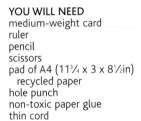
hole punch

thin cord

paper glue

scissors

card

recycled paper

1 To make the album cover, draw two rectangles measuring 15 x 3 x 22cm (6 x 3 x 8¾in) on the card. Cut them out.

2 Take twelve sheets of A4 recycled paper. Fold each sheet in half and carefully cut it along the fold to make two sheets of paper. Make a set of double holes in each sheet of paper with a hole punch.

3 Following the photograph, notch the corners of two sheets of recycled paper to decorate the album cover. Cut out the paper, and carefully stick each to one of the rectangles of card.

4 Cut two rectangles of contrasting paper measuring 21 x 3 x 14.5cm (8½ x 3 x 5¾in). Stick these to the inside front and back of the cover.

5 Punch holes in the covers, making sure that they correspond to those in the paper. Draw and cut out a simple cover motif from scraps of paper and stick them in place on the front of the album.

6 Align the covers and paper, and tie a small piece of cord through the top and bottom sets of holes. Make the cord loose enough to allow the pages to be turned over.

Corrugated Gift Tags

These unusual gift tags, although made from humble cardboard and string, look very stylish. They are especially suitable for gift wrapping items made from natural materials such as wood.

YOU WILL NEED
corrugated cardboard
ruler
pencil
scissors
decorative corrugated card
  in bright shades
non-toxic paper glue
hole punch
thick twine in a bright shade

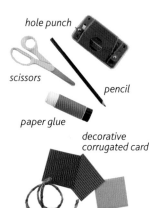

hole punch

scissors

pencil

paper glue

decorative
corrugated card

twine   cardboard

1 Draw label shapes measuring 9 x 3 x 6cm (3½ x 3 x 2¼in) on the corrugated cardboard. Cut them out using round-ended scissors.

2 Cut rectangles of decorative corrugated card slightly smaller than the gift tags. Stick them on the front of each tag.

3 Cut a zigzag shape from a piece of corrugated card in a contrasting shade and stick in place on top of the card rectangles.

4 With adult help, make a hole at the end of each label with a hole punch. Tie a length of twine through each hole.

Paper Gift Tags

What better way to jazz up a parcel then these cheerful gift tags? Make them in a variety of shades, wrap your parcels in bright, festive papers and parties will go with a swing.

YOU WILL NEED
heavy paper in a variety
    of shades
ruler
pencil
scissors
thin paper in a variety
    of shades
non-toxic paper glue
hole punch
bright cord

hole punch

ruler

pencil

scissors

paper

cord

1 Draw a rectangle measuring 14 x 3 x 8.5cm (5½ x 3 x 3¼in) on heavy bright paper and cut it out.

2 Draw an animal head on contrasting thin paper. Cut it out.

3 Divide the rectangle of paper in half. Draw a faint line down the middle of the paper and, with adult help, gently score along the line using a pair of scissors. Fold the card in half.

4 Stick the animal face to the front of the folded card with paper glue. With adult help, make a hole in the top left-hand corner of the back of the card with a hole punch. Tie a loop of cord through the hole.

Fancy Wrapped Parcels

Turn the humblest present into an exciting parcel by making the wrappings interesting and fun. All sorts of characters are appropriate for decorating parcels. Think of the person who will receive the parcel, and of their most-loved characters when choosing a design.

YOU WILL NEED
items to wrap
crêpe paper sheets
adhesive tape
paper ribbon
pencil
thin paper in a variety of shades
scissors
non-toxic paper glue
non-toxic strong glue

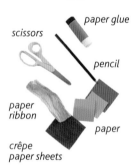

paper glue

scissors

pencil

paper
ribbon

paper

crêpe
paper sheets

1 Wrap the parcels neatly in some crêpe paper.

2 Open out lengths of paper ribbon and secure around each parcel.

3 Draw designs on to pieces of thin bright paper to make the head, arms and legs for each parcel (or head, legs and tail if an animal). Cut out the shapes.

4 Stick the decorative details on to each main body piece using some paper glue. Leave to dry.

5 Stick the decorations around the corners of each parcel with glue. You could make themed decorations, such as angels, snowmen and Santas.

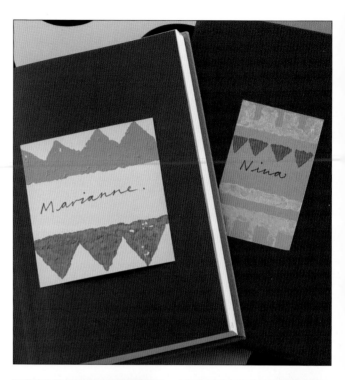

Bookplates

Some very beautiful bookplate designs have been produced for proud book-owners. Now you can make some for your own library. These are printed using blocks cut from scraps of polystyrene (Styrofoam). If the plates are fixed to the books using spray glue, they can be repositioned or removed as you please. You must ask an adult to cut the polystyrene for you – craft (utility) knives are very sharp.

YOU WILL NEED
small sheet of polystyrene 1.5cm
  (⅝in) thick
ruler
pencil
craft knife
non-toxic paint
paintbrush
heavy paper

paint

paintbrush

pencil *polystyrene*

ruler

paper

1 Draw a rectangle measuring 6 x 3 x 9cm (2¼ x 3 x 3½in) from a sheet of polystyrene. Ask an adult to cut out the rectangle for you using a craft knife.

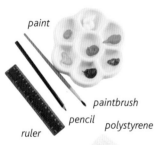

2 Draw a geometric design on one side of the rectangle. Ask an adult to cut around your design with a craft knife to leave a raised pattern.

3 Apply paint to the raised parts of the block with a paintbrush.

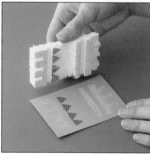

4 Press the block on to a rectangle of heavy paper. Apply pressure evenly to ensure good contact with the paper. Carefully remove the block, taking care not to smudge the paint. When the bookplate has dried, trim the paper to size.

Bookmarks

Don't lose your place! Remember where you are with these jolly bookmarks. They fit neatly over the top of the page so that you don't have to leaf through your book every time you want to catch up on some reading.

YOU WILL NEED
heavy purple and yellow paper
pencil
scissors
scraps of thin paper in
  bright shades
non-toxic paper glue

scissors

paper glue

pencil

paper

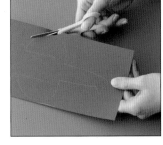

1 Draw a bird shape on the heavy purple paper and cut it out.

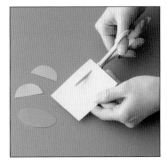

2 Draw the bird's beak, legs, wings and front on to appropriately toned pieces of paper. Cut them out.

3 Stick the bright details on to the front of the bird with paper glue.

4 Cut the giraffe bookmark from heavy yellow paper. Cut spots from orange paper and additional features from appropriately toned scraps and stick them in place.

Papier-mâché Necklace

*Papier-mâché is made by recycling old paper and cardboard;
why not carry on this ecological theme by decorating a
papier-mâché necklace with daisies and insects – you'll
blend in well at any garden party!*

YOU WILL NEED
large coin, for tracing circles
corrugated cardboard
pencil
scissors
newspaper
diluted non-toxic white glue
non-toxic white paint
paintbrush
non-toxic paint in a variety
  of shades
non-toxic clear gloss varnish
darning needle
non-toxic strong glue
eye pins
cord in a bright shade

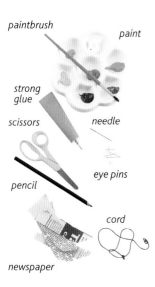

paintbrush

paint

strong glue

scissors

needle

pencil

eye pins

cord

newspaper

1 Place a round object such as a coin on the corrugated cardboard. Draw around it to make 12 discs and cut them out.

2 Cover each disc with three layers of thin papier-mâché strips. Leave them to dry overnight.

5 Seal each disc with two coats of gloss varnish. Once dry, with adult help, make a hole in the top of each with a needle. Dab strong glue over each hole and push in an eye pin.

3 Prime each cardboard disc with two coats of white paint and leave to dry completely.

6 Cut a long length of cord. Pass the cord through the eye pin of each disc and tie it before adding the next.

4 Draw a daisy or ladybird (ladybug) on each disc. Fill in the design with bright paints.

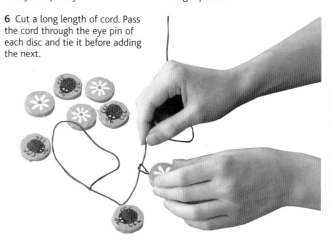

Papier-mâché Earrings

These earrings would make a good gift, and the beauty of papier-mâché is that however large the earrings, they won't weigh your ears down!

YOU WILL NEED
tracing paper
pencil
corrugated cardboard
scissors
newspaper
diluted non-toxic white glue
fine abrasive paper
non-toxic white paint
paintbrush
non-toxic paint in a variety
  of shades
non-toxic clear gloss varnish
darning needle
non-toxic strong glue
pair of eye pins
pliers
earring clips

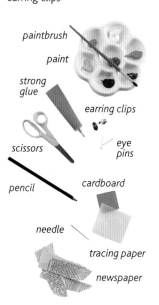

paintbrush

paint

strong
glue

earring clips

scissors

eye
pins

pencil

cardboard

needle

tracing paper

newspaper

1 Trace the earring pieces from the template and transfer to the cardboard twice. Cut them out.

2 Cover all the earring pieces in three layers of thin papier-mâché strips. Allow them to dry overnight.

3 Smooth the earring pieces with abrasive paper, then prime with two coats of white paint and leave to dry.

4 Decorate the earring pieces with bright paints and leave to dry.

5 Seal the dry earring pieces with two coats of gloss varnish.

6 With adult help, make a small hole in each piece with the darning needle. Dab a little strong glue over each hole and push an eye pin into each. Leave the glue to dry. With adult help, use pliers to open the loops of the eye pins in the lower half of each earring. Hook the lower to the upper half, and close the loops. Use strong glue to attach the earring clips and allow to dry thoroughly before wearing.

Papier-mâché Brooch

Animal designs make good brooches; you could also make earrings to match these two jolly creatures. The brooch backs are known as 'findings' and can be bought from craft, hobby and bead stores.

YOU WILL NEED
tracing paper
pencil
corrugated cardboard
scissors
newspaper
diluted non-toxic white glue
fine abrasive paper
paintbrush
non-toxic white paint
non-toxic paint in a variety
  of shades
non-toxic clear gloss varnish
brooch fastening
non-toxic strong glue

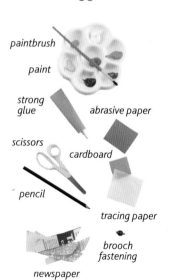

paintbrush

paint

strong
glue

abrasive paper

scissors

cardboard

pencil

tracing paper

brooch
fastening

newspaper

1 Trace or scale up the cat template from the beginning of the book, or draw your own. Transfer the design to cardboard and cut it out.

2 Cover the cat with three layers of thin papier-mâché strips. Allow to dry thoroughly.

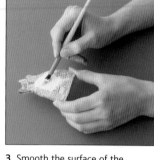

3 Smooth the surface of the brooch with fine abrasive paper, then paint it with white paint and leave to dry.

4 Draw in the cat's features, and then decorate the brooch with paint and a fine paintbrush.

5 When the paint is thoroughly dry, seal the brooch with two coats of gloss varnish. Leave to dry.

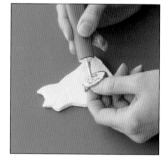

6 Attach a brooch fastening to the back of the cat with strong glue. Let the brooch dry overnight before you wear it. Any number of other designs of your choice may be made in the same way.

Stationery Folder in Fancy Paper

These folders would make welcome presents for an avid correspondent. They can be labelled by subject or name to make a useful filing system.

YOU WILL NEED
decorative paper
ruler
pencil
scissors
non-toxic paper glue

scissors

paper glue

pencil

paper

1 On the wrong side of the decorative paper measure and draw a rectangle 32 x 3 x 47cm (12½ x 3 x 18½in). Cut it out.

2 Following the template at the beginning of the book, mark out the folder on the wrong side of the rectangle of paper.

3 Cut out the top notch and flap from the folder.

4 Fold the side panels to the middle of the folder and stick them together. Fold the bottom flap over the side panels and stick it in place.

Letter File

Important and treasured letters should be saved, and a letter file is the perfect container. Illustrate yours with vibrant cut-outs for a stylish effect.

YOU WILL NEED
heavy paper
ruler
pencil
scissors
non-toxic paper glue
scraps of thin paper in
   bright shades

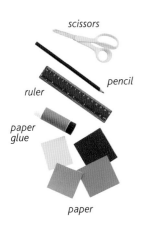

scissors

ruler   pencil

paper
glue

paper

1 Measure and draw a rectangle 47 x 3 x 32cm (18½ x 3 x 12½in) on heavy bright paper. Cut it out.

2 Following the diagram, mark up the rectangle to form the file. Cut away the excess paper and stick the side panels together in the middle. Stick the base flap over the bottom of the side panels.

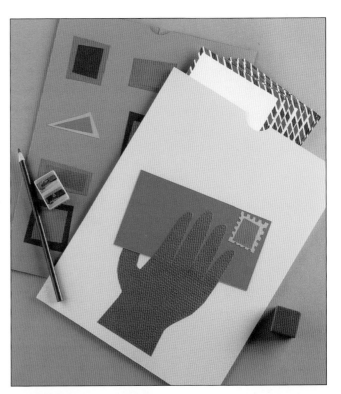

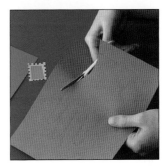

3 Cut out a hand motif from red paper. Cut an asymmetrical rectangle from blue paper to represent an envelope. Cut the stamp from yellow and orange scraps.

4 Carefully stick the cut-outs to the front of the letter file and leave to dry. You can make additional files in the same way, decorated with your own designs.

Foil-covered Frame

Do you have a preferred photograph or picture that deserves a special frame? Why not make one in papier-mâché? This one looks very impressive with its bright foil surface and will take standard-sized photographs.

YOU WILL NEED
graph paper
thick and thin corrugated
  cardboard
pencil
ruler
scissors
non-toxic strong glue
newspaper
diluted non-toxic white glue
paintbrush
non-toxic white paint
silver foil
foil in bright shades
2 picture hangers
thin cord

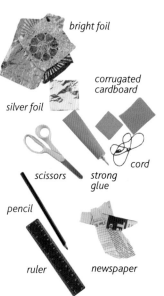

bright foil

corrugated
cardboard

silver foil

cord

scissors

strong
glue

pencil

ruler   newspaper

1 Scale up each piece of frame from the template at the beginning of the book on to appropriate cardboard. The front and back frame should be drawn on to thick cardboard, and the spacer on thin. Cut out each piece.

2 Stick the spacer to the frame front with strong glue.

3 Cover both sections with three layers of papier-mâché strips. Allow the frame to dry overnight in a warm place.

4 Prime the dry frame pieces with white paint. Although the paint won't be seen it will be easier to see where to stick the foil if the surface of the frame is white. Allow the paint to dry completely.

5 Cover the frame pieces with silver foil. Stick the frame front to the back. Cover the joins with strips of foil.

6 Cut small circles of bright foil and stick them around the frame in a pleasing arrangement. Stick the hangers to the back of the frame with strong glue, and add the cord to hang the frame.

Papier-mâché Mirror Frame

This twinkling mirror frame will create a sparkling focal point in any room. It is decorated with a variety of interesting sequins, but other objects such as vibrant buttons, bottle tops and small shaped buttons would be just as good.

YOU WILL NEED
tracing paper or graph paper
corrugated cardboard
pencil
ruler
scissors
masking tape
2 picture hangers
newspaper
diluted non-toxic white glue
paintbrush
non-toxic white paint
non-toxic bright paint
non-toxic strong glue
sequins
non-toxic clear gloss varnish
12 x 3 x 12cm (4³⁄₄ x 3 x 4³⁄₄in)
   mirror tile
thin cord

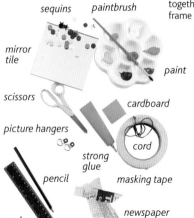

sequins
paintbrush
mirror tile
paint
scissors
cardboard
picture hangers
cord
strong glue
pencil
masking tape
ruler
newspaper

1 Trace or scale up the mirror frame pieces from the template and transfer to heavy cardboard. Cut them out.

2 Use masking tape to stick the front and back of the frame together. Stick the hangers to the frame back with masking tape.

3 Cover the entire frame with three layers of papier-mâché, avoiding the metal hangers. Leave the frame to dry overnight in a warm place.

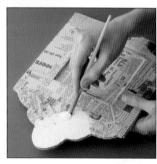

4 Prime the frame with two coats of white paint. Leave to dry.

5 Add two coats of bright paint. Stick the sequins around the frame. Varnish with a coat of clear varnish.

6 Stick the mirror tile in place. Tie a cord through the metal hangers on the back of the frame.

INDEX

ACKNOWLEDGEMENTS
The author would like to thank James Duncan for taking great photographs; Lucy Sykes for appearing in the book; Madeleine Brehaut for letting us raid her props; and Lindsay Porter for her help styling the finished pictures.